MUSIC OF THE STARS

RARE JAZZ AND POPULAR SONGS FROM THE AMERICAN SONGBOOK

Songs Recorded by
DIANA KRALL

T0087250

As Long As I Live
by Harold Arlen and Ted Koehler.. 6

Baby, Baby All The Time
by Bobby Troup... 2

Better Than Anything
by Bill Loughborough and David Wheat................................... 12

Between The Devil And The Deep Blue Sea
by Harold Arlen and Ted Koehler.. 16

Blue Gardenia
by Bob Russell and Lester Lee... 20

Body And Soul
by E. Heyman, R. Sour, F. Eyton and J. Green....................... 22

Do It Again!
by George Gershwin and Buddy DeSylva............................... 26

Do Nothin' Till You Hear From Me
by Duke Ellington and Bob Russell.. 29

(The) Frim Fram Sauce
by Redd Evans and Joe Ricardel... 32

(A) Garden In The Rain
by James Dyrenforth and Carroll Gibbons............................. 36

If I Had You
by Ted Shapiro, Jimmy Campbell and Reg Connelly............... 44

I Should Care
by Sammy Cahn, Axel Stordahl and Paul Weston................... 41

I've Got The World On A String
by Harold Arlen and Ted Koehler.. 54

Maybe You'll Be There
by Sammy Gallop and Rube Bloom....................................... 56

(The) Night We Called It A Day
by Matt Dennis and Tom Adair... 50

When The Sun Comes Out
by Harold Arlen and Ted Koehler.. 5

Produced by JOHN L. HAAG

Sales and Shipping:

PROFESSIONAL MUSIC INSTITUTE LLC
1336 Cruzero Street, Box 128, Ojai, CA 93024
info@promusicbooks.com

Baby, Baby All The Time

Lyric and Music by
Bobby Troup

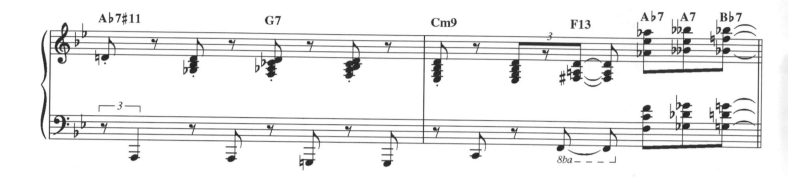

1. Once I had a man,
(Verses 2 & 3 see block lyrics)
sweet as he could be.

Once I had a man and he was right for me. __

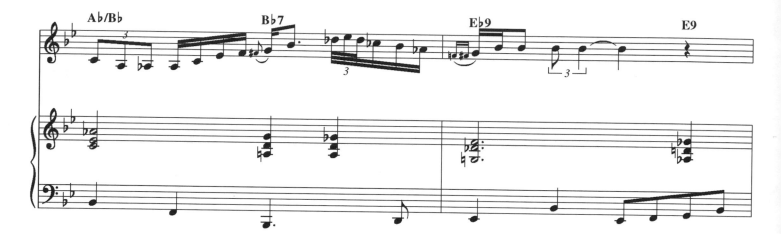

4

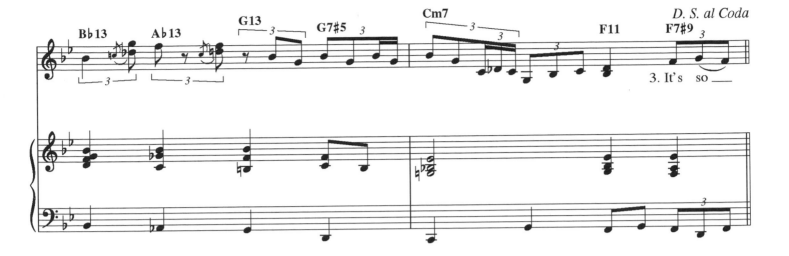

Verse 2:

He said baby can't you see
Baby understand
Baby you're for me
Oh, won't you take my hand?
But I pushed him away
Wouldn't let him near
Pushed him far away
And now I'm wishing
I could hear him call me baby
Baby all the time.

Verse 3:

It's so lonely through the day
Lonely through the night
Lonely, lonely hours without
That man I held so tight
Lord I pray that you
Will listen to my plea
Keep him close to you
So he'll come back to me
And call me baby
Baby all the time.

As Long As I Live

Lyric by Ted Koehler
Music by Harold Arlen

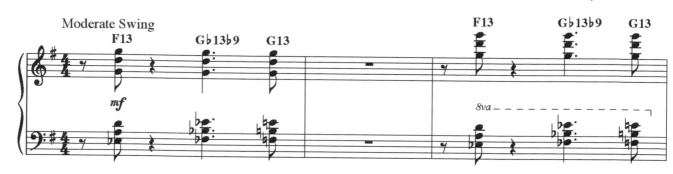

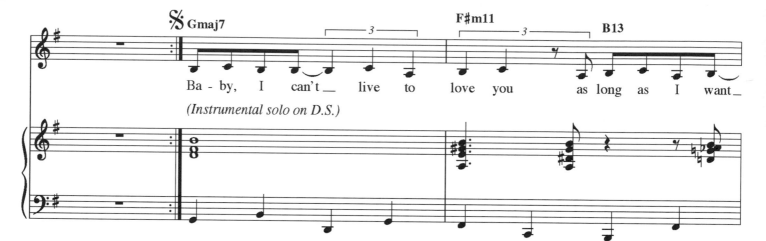

Ba - by, I can't __ live to love you as long as I want __

(Instrumental solo on D.S.)

__ to. __ Life __ is - n't long e-nough, ba - by, __

but I can love you as long as I live. __

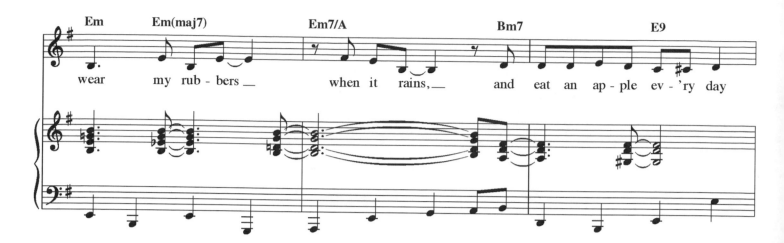

Page 9

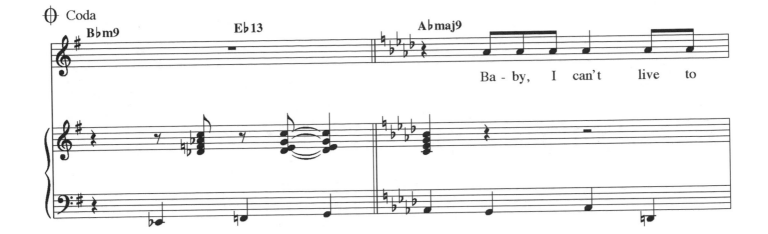

As long as I live 4-7

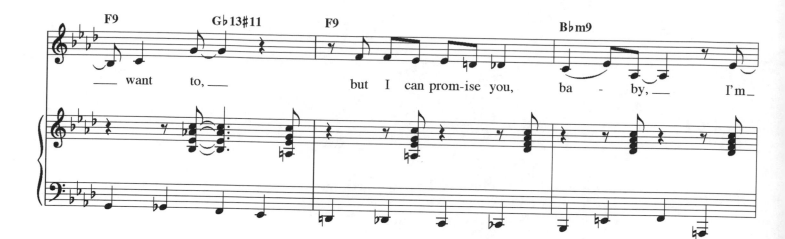

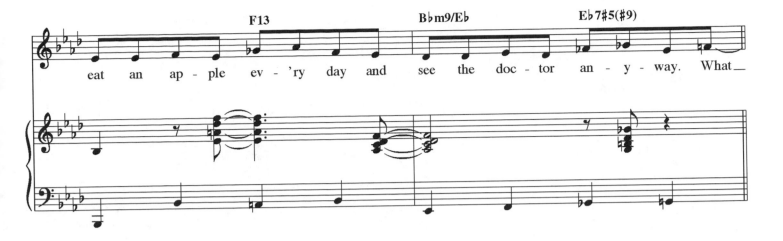

As long as I live 6-7

12

As long as I live 7-7

Better Than Anything

Lyric by Bill Loughborough
Music by David Wheat

Jazz Waltz Feel

Between The Devil And
The Deep Blue Sea

Lyric by Ted Koehler
Music by Harold Arlen

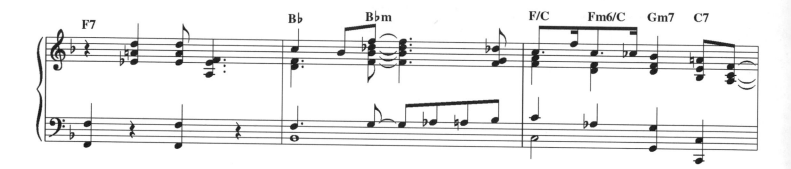

(last time) Is there an - y - one a-round

who can not see it's the wellknown run - a - round you're giv - ing me,

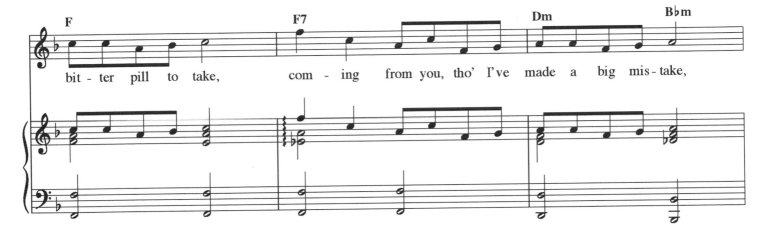

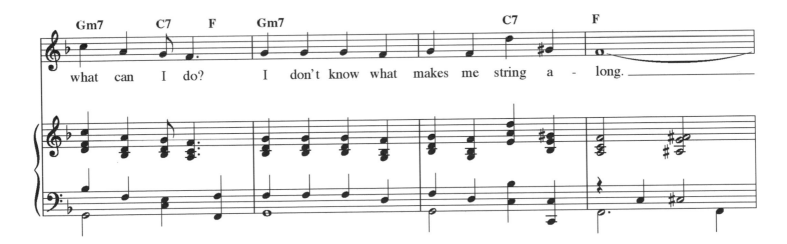

Between the devil and the deep blue sea 2-4

18

Between the devil and the deep blue sea 3-4

but when you come knock-ing at my door. __ Fate seems to give my

heart a twist, __ and I come run-ning back for more. I should

hate you but I guess I love you. You've got me

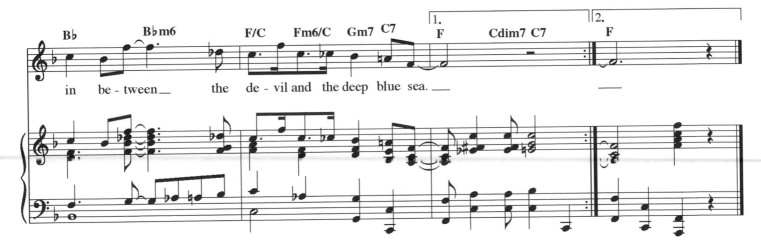

in be - tween __ the de - vil and the deep blue sea. __

Between the devil and the deep blue sea 4-4

Blue Gardenia

Lyric and Music by
Bob Russell and Lester Lee

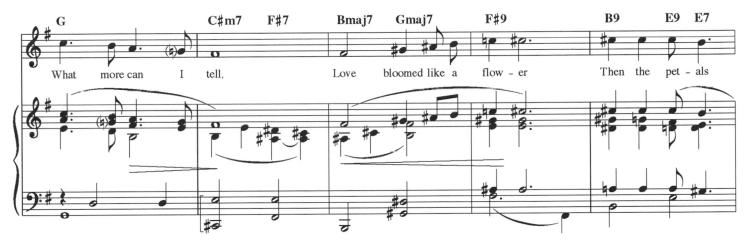

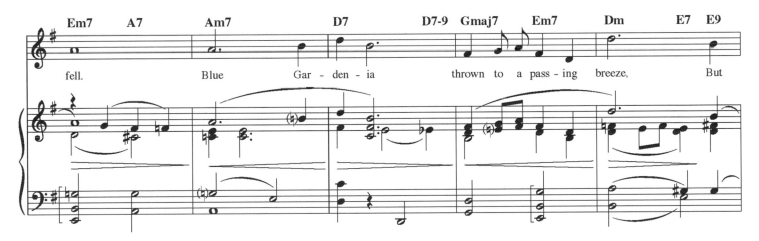

Blue Gardenia 2-2

Body And Soul

Lyric by Edward Heyman, Robert Sour and Frank Eyton
Music by John Green

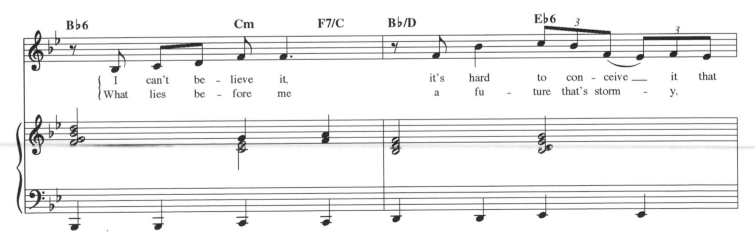

Body and soul 2-4

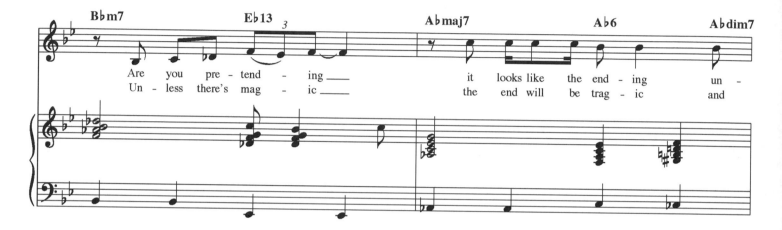

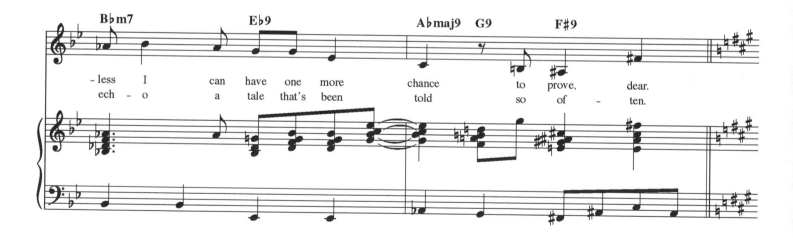

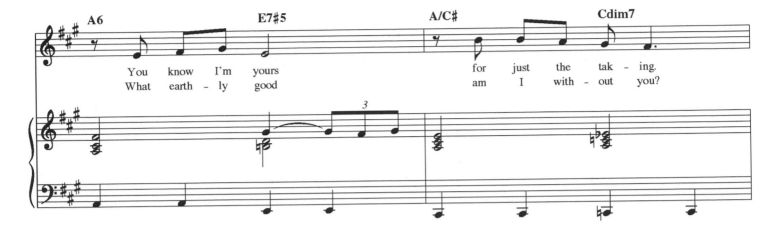

You know I'm yours for just the tak - ing.
What earth - ly good am I with - out you?

1.

I'd glad - ly sur - ren - der ____
I tell you I

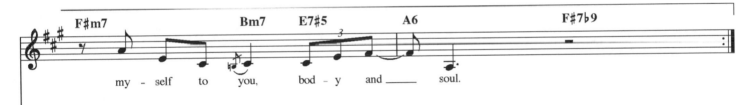

my - self to you, bod - y and ____ soul.

2.

mean it. I'm all for you, bod - y and soul. _____

Do It Again!

Lyric by Buddy DeSylva
Music by George Gershwin

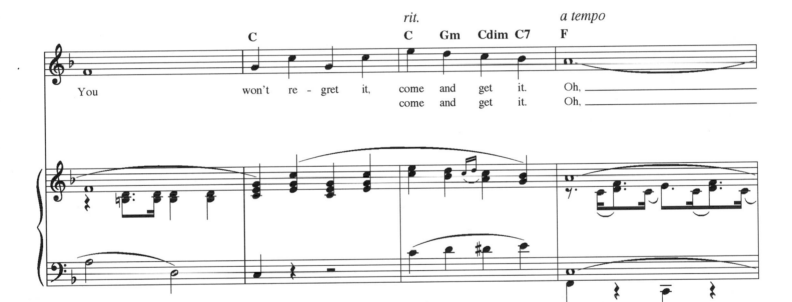

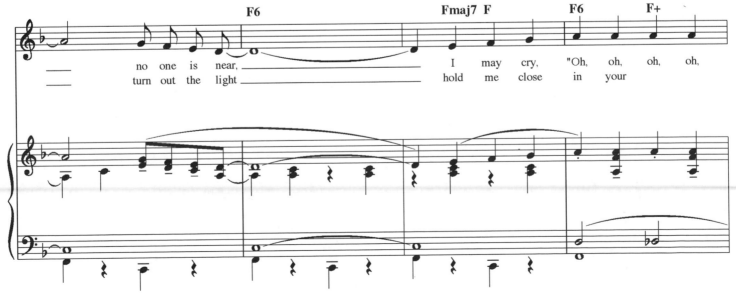

Do it again! 2-3

28

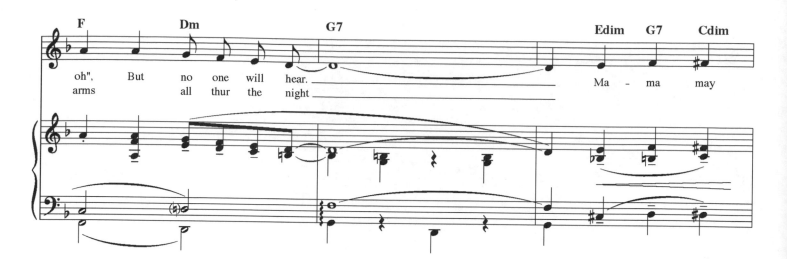

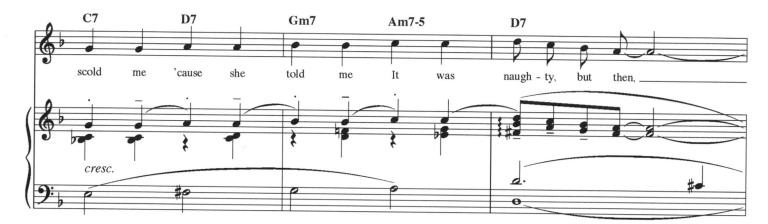

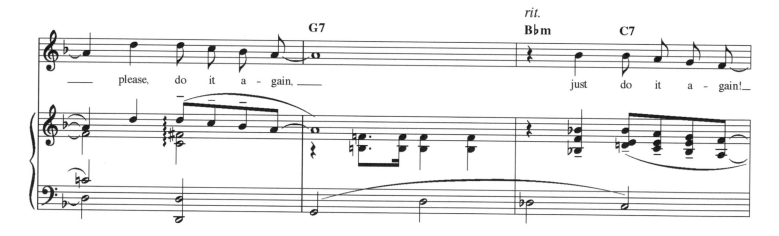

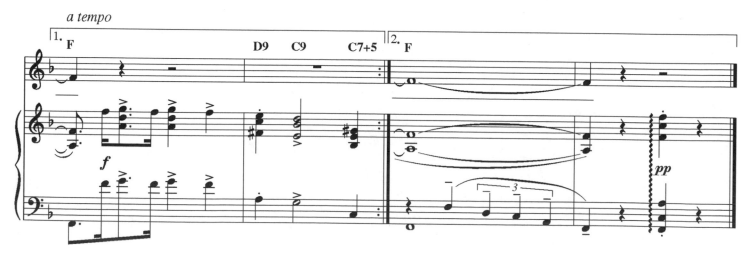

Do it again! 3-3

Do Nothin' Till You Hear From Me

Lyric by Bob Russell
Music by Duke Ellington

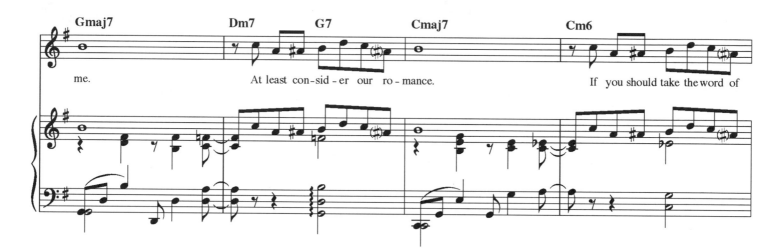

Do nothin' till you hear from me 2-3

31

Do nothin' till you hear from me 3-3

The Frim Fram Sauce

Lyric and Music by
Joe Ricardel and Redd Evans

I don't want french fried po-ta-toes, red __
Instrumental solo

__ ripe to-ma-toes, _ I'm nev-er sat-is-fied. __ I want the

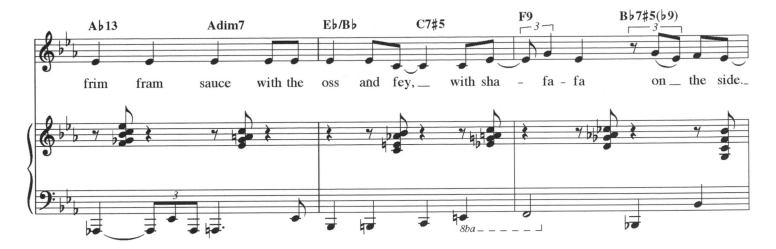

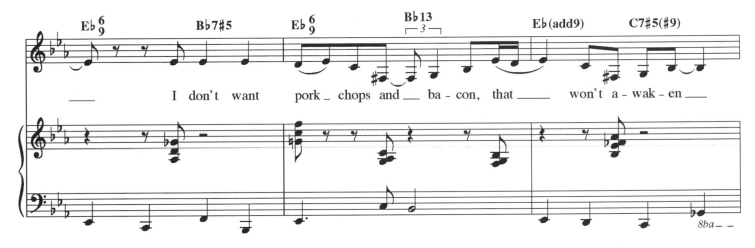

The frim fram sauce 2–4

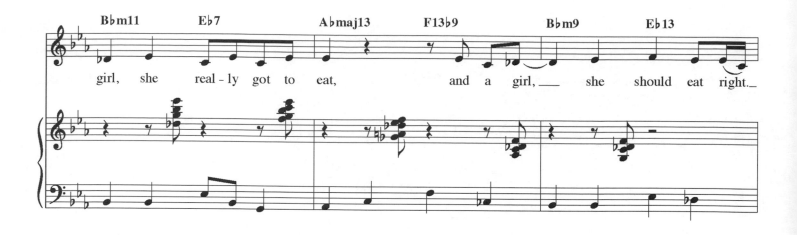

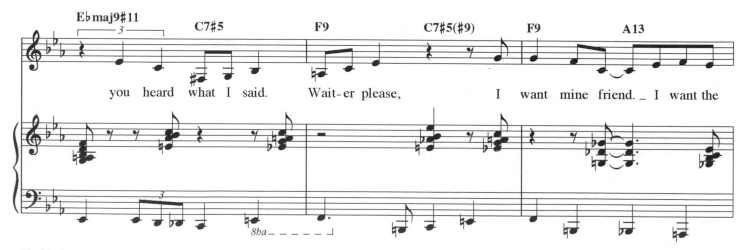

frim fram _ sauce with the oss and fey, _ with sha - fa - fa on __ the side.

(2nd time) I don't want

Ooh, with sha - fa - fa _____ on __ the side. _

The frim fram sauce 4-4

Garden In The Rain

Lyric by James Dyrenforth
Music by Carroll Gibbons

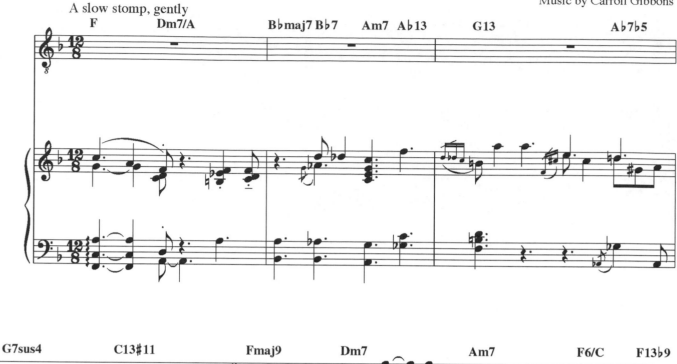

'Twas just a gar-den in the rain, _

close to a lit-tle leaf-y lane, _ a touch of col-our

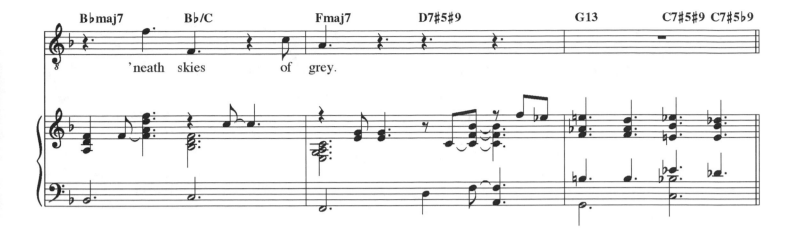

Garden in the rain 2-5

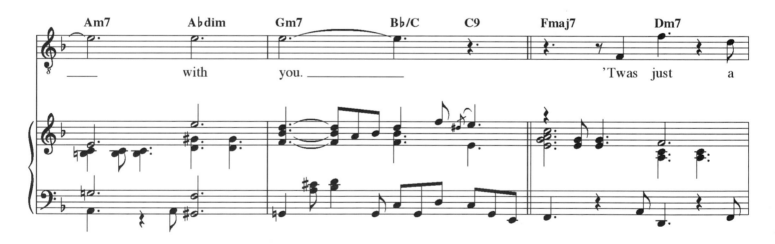

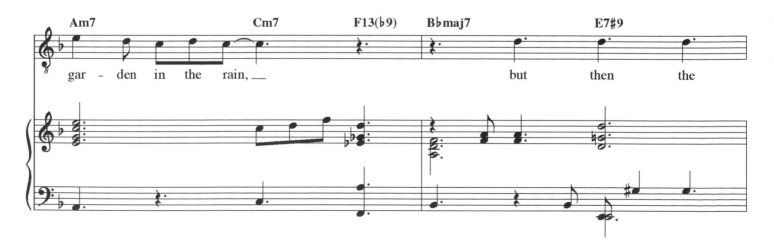

Garden in the rain 3-5

sun came out a- gain, ___ and sent us hap - pi -

To Coda ⊕

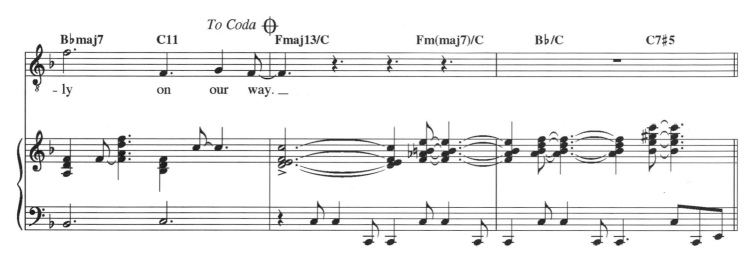

- ly on our way. ___

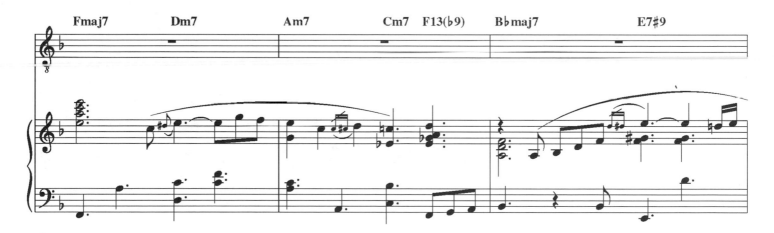

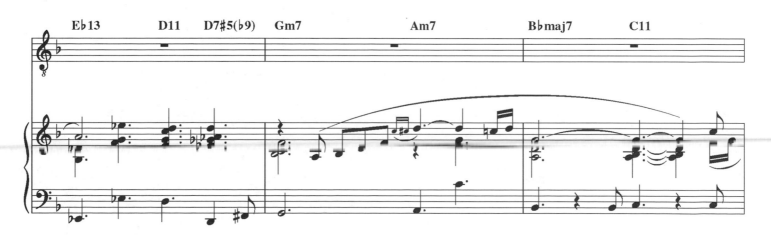

Garden in the rain 4-5

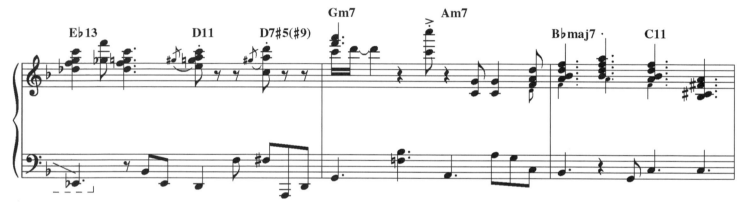

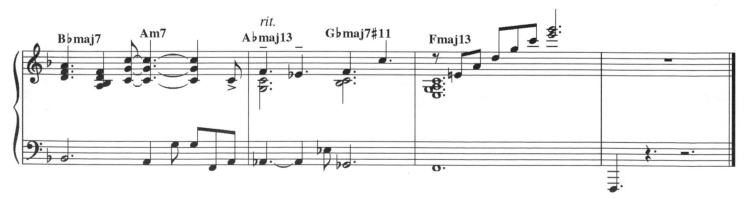

Garden in the rain 5-5

I Should Care

Lyric and Music by
Sammy Cahn, Axel Stordahl and Paul Weston

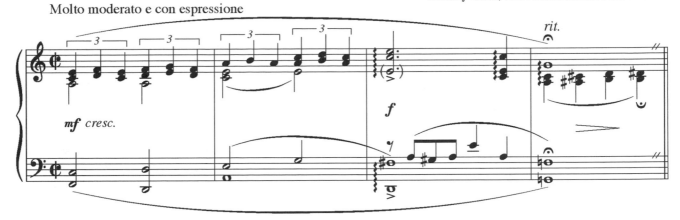

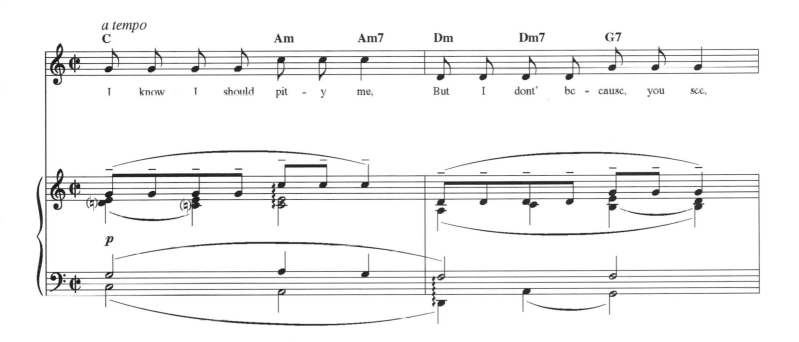

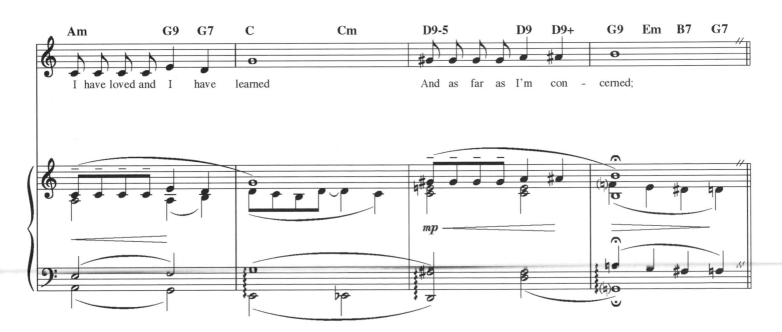

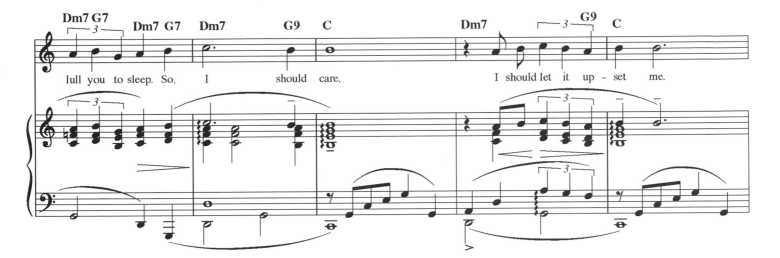

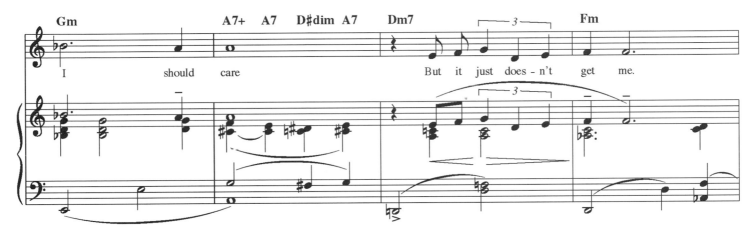

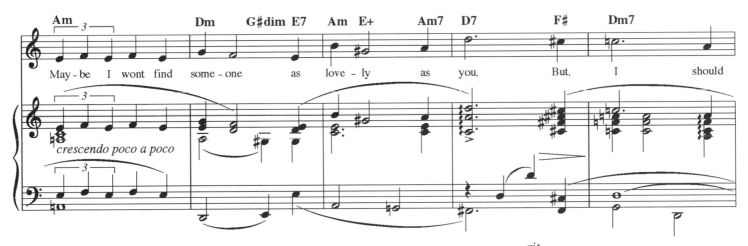

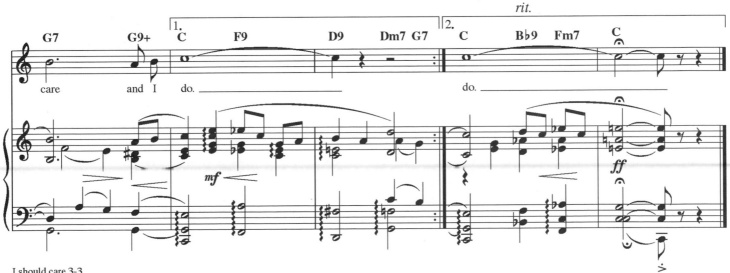

I should care 3-3

If I Had You

Lyric and Music by
Ted Shapiro, Jimmy Campbell & Reg Connelly

I could show the world _ how to smile, I could be

glad all of the while, I could turn the grey skies to

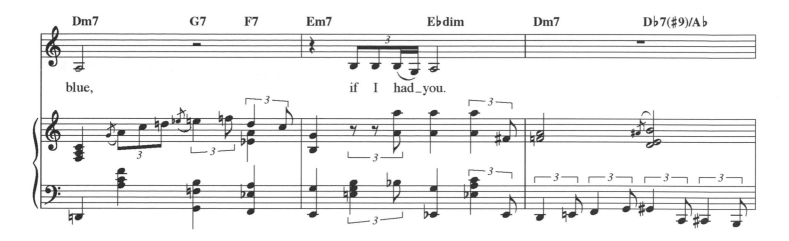

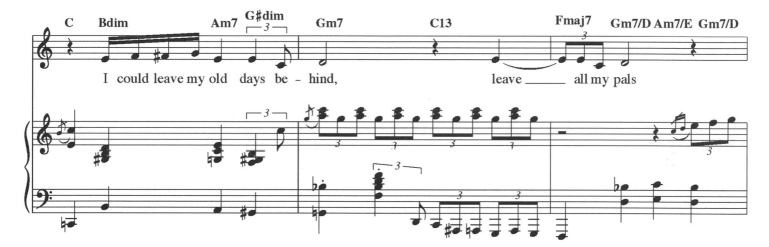

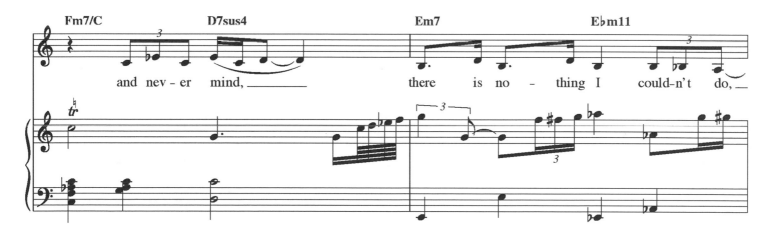

If I had you 2-7

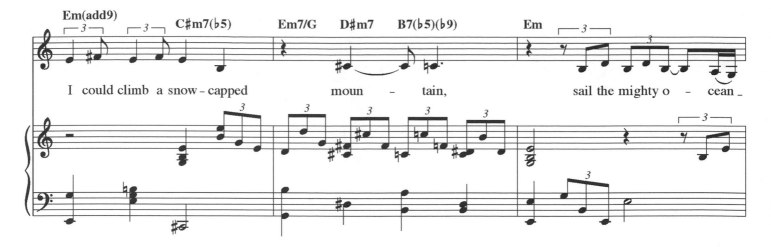

I could climb a snow - capped moun - tain, sail the mighty o - cean _

wide, _____ I could cross a burn - ing des - ert,

if I had you by ___ my side. ___ I could be a queen _ dear un-

-crowned, hum-ble or _ poor, rich or re-nowned,

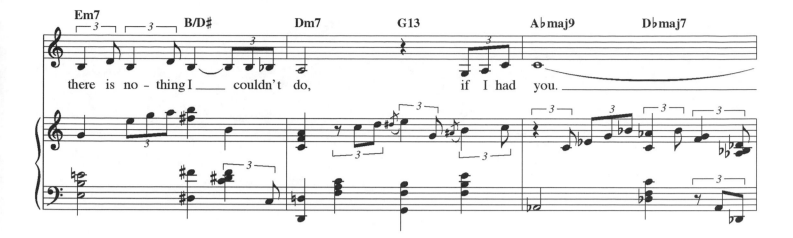

there is no - thing I ____ couldn't do, if I had you. ____

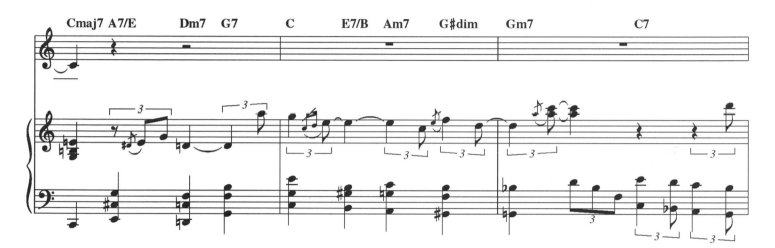

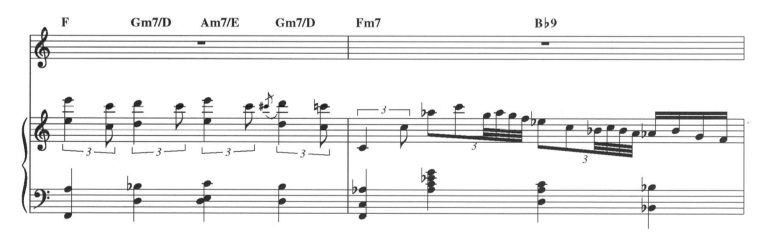

If I had you 4-7

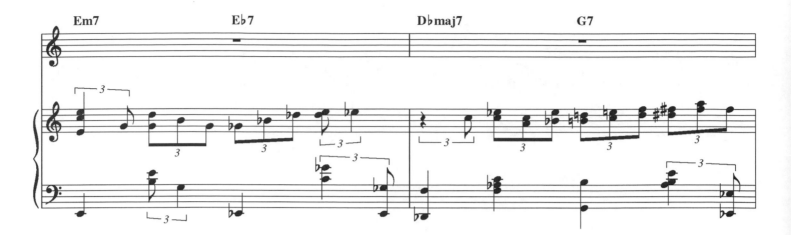

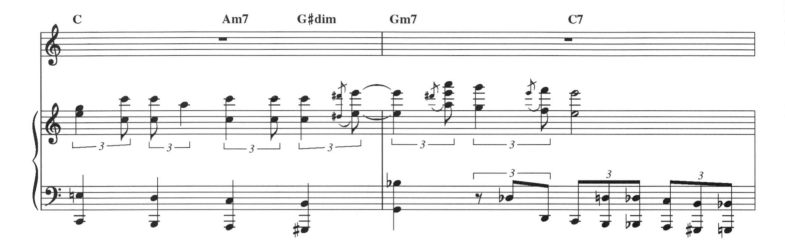

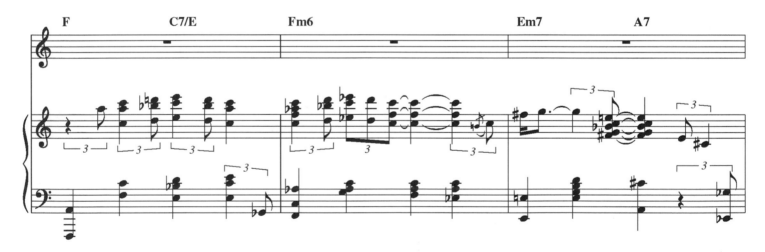

If I had you 5-7

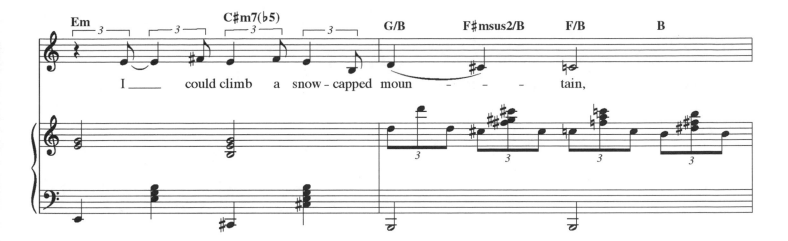

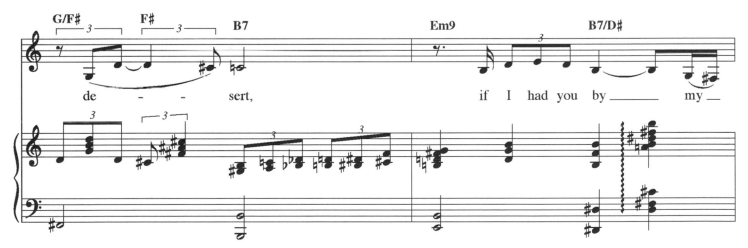

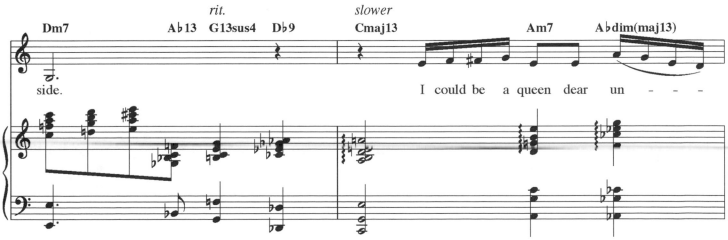

If I had you 6-7

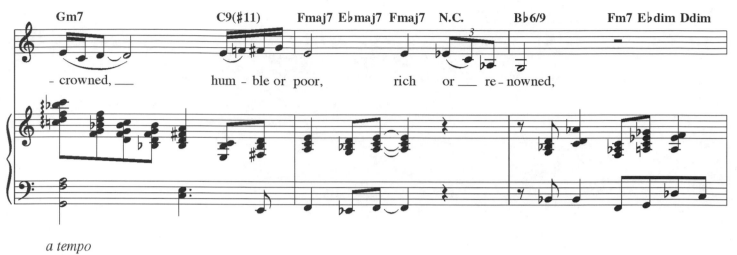

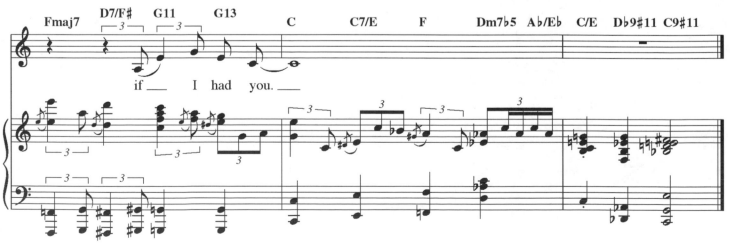

When the Sun Comes Out

Lyric by Ted Koehler
Music by Harold Arlen

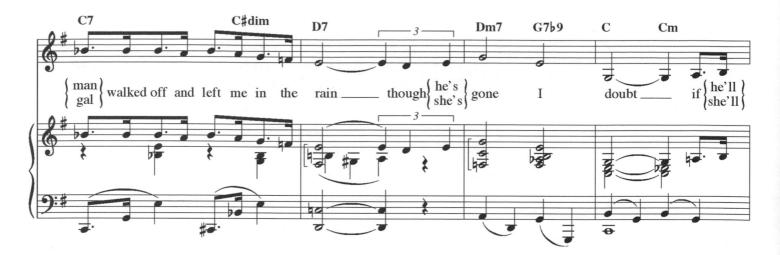

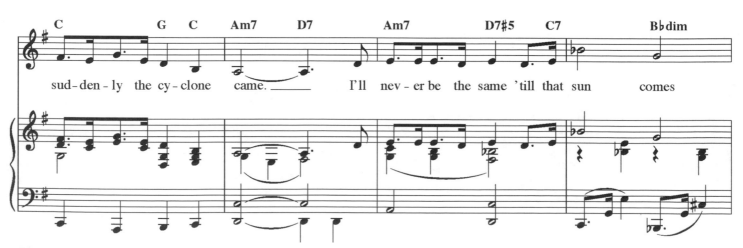

When the sun comes out 3-3

I've Got The World On A String

Lyric by Ted Koehler
Music by Harold Arlen

Swing Tempo

I've got the

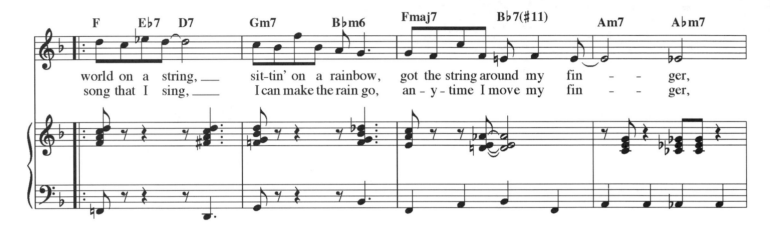

world on a string, ___ sit-tin' on a rainbow, got the string around my fin - - ger,
song that I sing, ___ I can make the rain go, an - y - time I move my fin - - ger,

what a world, what a ___ life, I'm in love. I've got a
luck - y me, can't you ___ see I'm in

love. _____ Life is a beauti-ful thing, ___ as long as I hold the string,

I'd be a sil-ly so and so if I should ev-er let go.

I've got the world on a string,__ sit-tin' on a rainbow,

got the string around my fin - - ger, what a world, what a __ life, I'm in

love. _____

I've got the world on a string 2-2

Maybe You'll Be There

Lyric by Sammy Gallop
Music by Rube Bloom

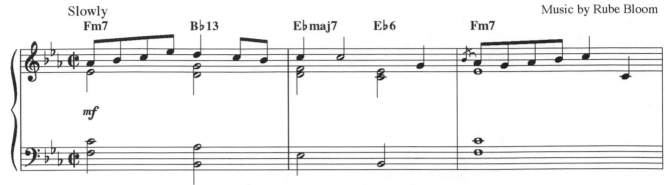

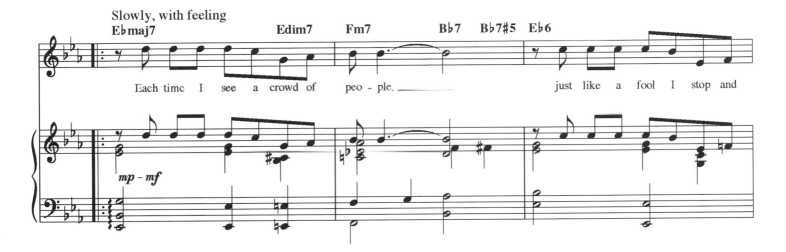

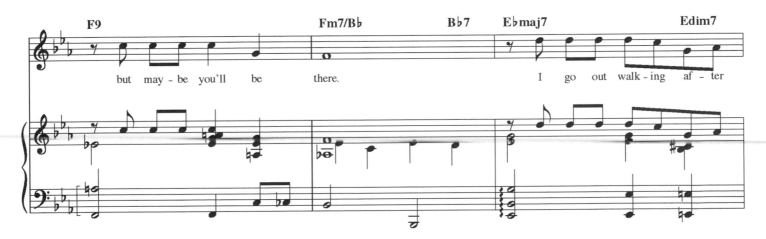

Maybe you'll be there 2-4

Maybe you'll be there 3-4

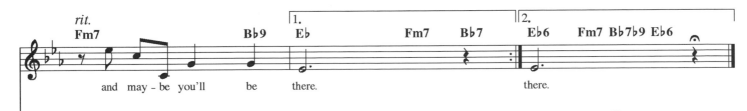

Maybe you'll be there 4-4

The Night We Called It A Day

Lyric by Tom Adair
Music by Matt Dennis

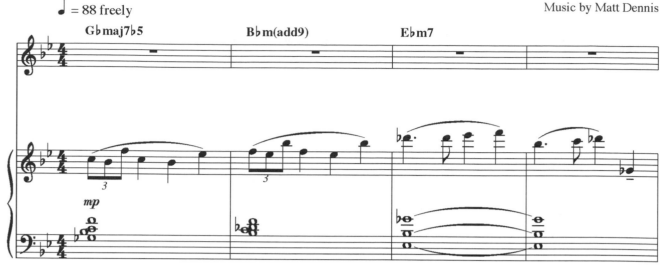

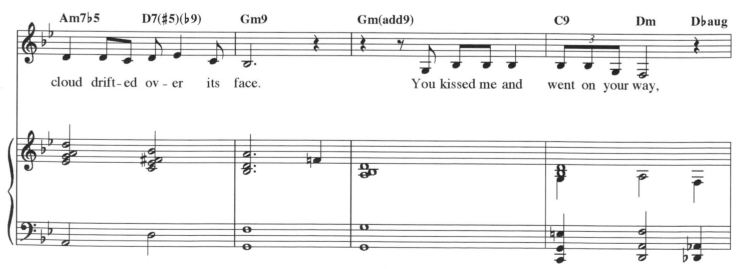

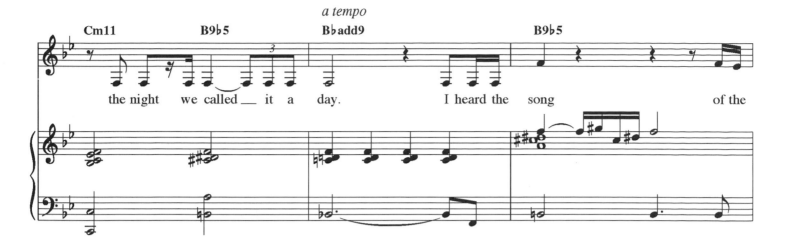

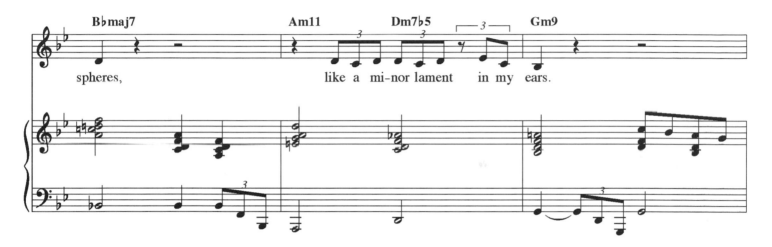

The night we called it a day 2-5

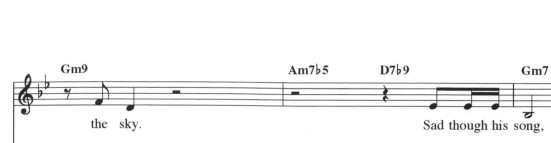

the sky.   Sad though his song,

no blu-er was he _____ than I.   The moon went down and stars were

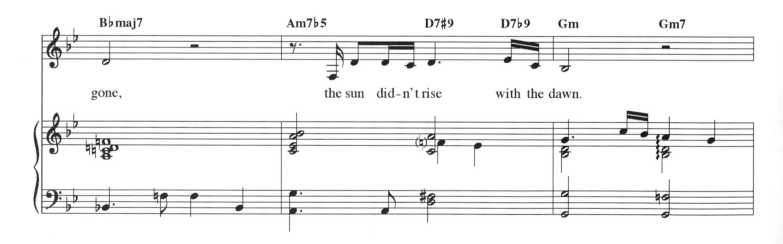

gone,   the sun did-n't rise   with the dawn.

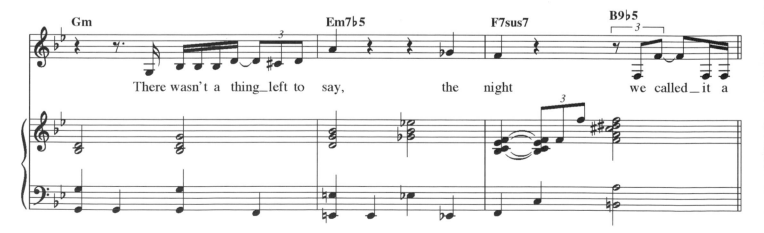

There wasn't a thing left to say,   the   night   we called it a

The night we called it a day 3-5

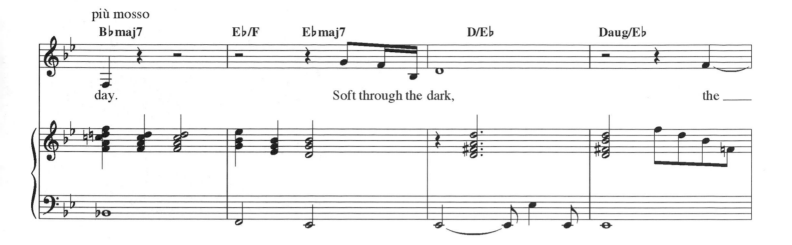

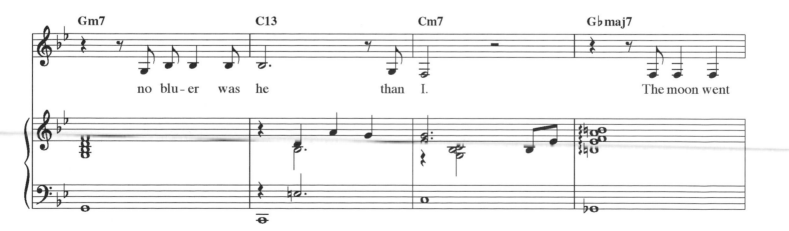

The night we called it a day 4-5

64

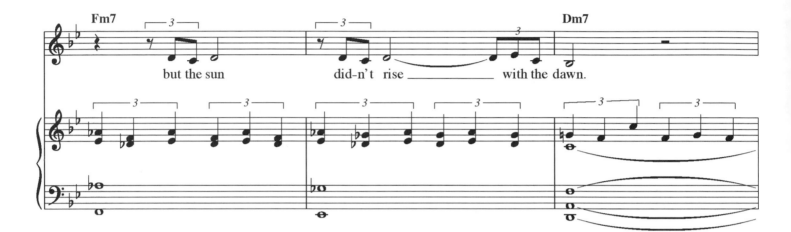

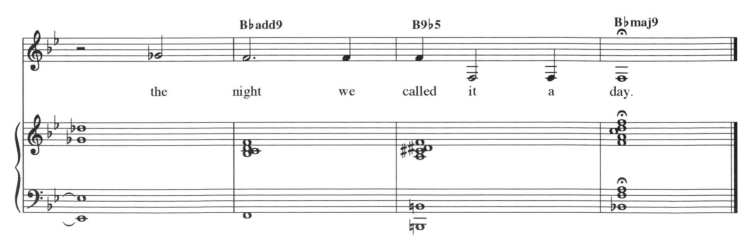

The night we called it a day 5-5